W9-BNB-404

Mathew,
Thank you
Cyndi

serenity
prayers

serenity prayers

Prayers, Poems, and Prose to Soothe Your Soul

June Cotner

Andrews McMeel
Publishing®

a division of Andrews McMeel Universal

Andrews McMeel Publishing
a division of Andrews McMeel Universal
1130 Walnut Street, Kansas City, Missouri 64106

www.andrewsmcmeel.com

16 17 18 19 20 WKT 10 9 8 7 6 5 4 3

ISBN: 978-1-4494-4602-4

Library of Congress Control Number: 2014939484

ATTENTION: SCHOOLS AND BUSINESSES

Andrews McMeel books are available at quantity discounts with
bulk purchase for educational, business, or sales promotional use.
For information, please e-mail the Andrews McMeel Publishing
Special Sales Department: specialsales@amuniversal.com.

Serenity Prayers is dedicated to
my dear friend Anna Johnson,
who gave me the idea for this book!

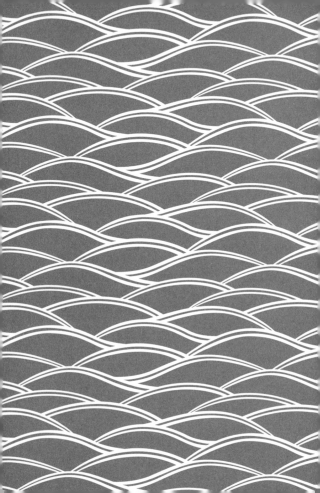

CONTENTS

Thanks xi

Letter to Readers xv

one

SERENITY 1

Joy 2

Welcoming Angels 4

A Clear Midnight 5

Let Us Spend One Day as Deliberately as Nature 6

An Ordinary Day 7

I Must Walk Again the Wooded Path 8

The Gift I Give Myself 10

When I Dance, I Dance 12

Drop Thy Still Dews of Quietness 13

Listen 14

Be Still 15

Mining the Heart 16

Serenity Is Not 18

two

FAITH 19

When I'm Weary 20

Angel Embrace 22

Win or Lose, I Will Survive 24

You Must Believe 25

Renewal 26

Consolation 27

The Kaleidoscope of Life 28
Let Nothing Disturb You 29
Prayer for Protection 30

three

COURAGE AND HOPE 31
Living in Hope 32
Hope 34
Contentment's Recipe 35
Climbing the Jade Mountain 36
Building Bravery 38
Yes 39
Seeds 40

four

RELAXATION 41
Sometimes, in a Summer Morning 42
Let Your Soul Create a Sanctuary 43
Windchimes 44
No Hurry 45
Sanctuary 46
How the Rose Works 48
Hammock 50

five

REFLECTIONS 51
Chasseurcistic 52
The World We Make 54
Success 56

Forgiveness 57

Is It So Small a Thing 58

Passion 59

Requiem for My Sister 60

The Lame Goat 62

Of Consequence 64

It Will Pass 66

Unconditional Dividends 67

I Saw That It Was Good 68

Realizations 70

Enigma 72

Clouds That Pass 73

The Songs Along the Way 74

six

JOY AND GRATITUDE 75

The Cup of Life 76

Listen, 78

Nevertheless; 80

Humility 82

Gravy 84

Precious Moments 86

Take Nothing for Granted 88

Dawn's Grace 90

My Beautiful Day 91

Going Through the Motions 92

Gratitude 94

No Longer Forward nor Behind 95

Invocation 96

Everyday Blessings 98

seven

PRAYERS 99

Psalm for the Meaning of Life 100
Live Quietly 101
Poet's Compline 102
Hindu Prayer 103
A Prayer of Thanksgiving 104
Prayer for Perspective 106
On This Day 107
I Pray Today 108

eight

INSPIRATION 109

My Symphony 110
Epiphany 111
The Way Home 112
Tomorrow Is Not Promised 115
The Journey 116
Writer's Colony, Spring 118
I Can Believe in Fairies 120
As If Forever . . . 122
I Believe 124
It's All Good 126
The Gift 128
Pippa's Song 129

Author Index 131
Permissions and Acknowledgments 133
About the Author 136

THANKS

The idea for *Serenity Prayers* came about when I was talking with my friend Anna Johnson about my prayers and blessings books. Anna was feeling particularly frazzled and said, "I could use something called *Serenity Prayers* right now!" Thank you, Anna! Here it is.

I was excited about the possibility of creating a book in which the selections would actually help us feel more serene and at peace within ourselves and our circumstances. I sent out a call for submissions to my nine hundred–plus regular contributors and placed an ad in *Poets and Writers*.

Initially, I considered more than three thousand submissions for *Serenity Prayers* and found many other possible selections from my extensive library of inspiring books. I narrowed down my favorites to two hundred selections. I knew that the final book would contain a little over one hundred selections; truly, I had a good problem— too many great selections! My deepest thanks go to the contributing poets to my anthologies. Without you, my books wouldn't be possible. I wish there were room to include all of your excellent pieces!

The living writers who submitted for this book, as well as the writers who are no longer with us, all leave an indelible trace of wonder, beauty, and poignancy in our world. They are the souls who are gifted with the ability to translate spiritual experiences into a language that speaks to everyone. As an anthologist, I'm grateful to be their conduit, bringing their words to the printed page.

In my daily life I still find myself in awe of the synchronicity that brings me to possible selections for my books, whether it's an obscure poem in a vintage book given to me by my cousin Margie or something I simply stumble upon. For example, the quote by Mitch Albom on page 7 appeared on a plaque commemorating the life of a hiker, at the top of a peak in the Olympic Mountains. The poem by Matthew Arnold on page 58 is something I've kept since my college years—and here it is, forty years later, appearing in one of my collections.

I feel especially blessed by the joys of my family: my husband, Jim Graves; my daughter, Kirsten Casey; my son, Kyle Myrvang; and dear relatives in my extended family, who all support me in myriad ways.

My heartfelt gratitude goes to my dedicated agents, Denise Marcil and Anne Marie O'Farrell at Marcil-O'Farrell Literary LLC; my editor, Patty Rice, and all the folks at Andrews McMeel who worked on *Serenity Prayers*.

And finally, I'm grateful to God for bringing talented writers, wonderful friends and family, and countless blessings to my life.

LETTER TO READERS

God grant me the serenity
to accept the things I cannot change,
courage to change the things I can
and wisdom to know the difference.

I have frequently turned to "The Serenity Prayer" throughout my life. It's one of the most revered messages of our time and has touched countless lives.

Many circumstances in modern life affect our sense of peace and contentment—stressful jobs, relationship difficulties, day-to-day worries, and a sense of feeling overwhelmed with the hyperspeed demands of life. In *Serenity Prayers,* I've offered helpful thoughts, perspectives, and insights that encourage us to create more peace, joy, and tranquillity in our lives.

The pathway to serenity most often includes strong faith, which keeps us calm even in the midst of excitement, adversity, or danger. Our faith leads us toward courage to endeavor to overcome our difficulties while continuing to believe in the goodness and great meaning of life. Before including a passage in *Serenity Prayers*, I asked myself, "Does this selection make me feel more serene, open doors to faith and courage, offer a needed perspective, or help me feel more joy and gratitude?"

In *Serenity Prayers*, the voices of classic visionaries such as Rumi, Henry David Thoreau, and Walt Whitman mingle with fresh thoughts of contemporary writers such as Mitch Albom and Barbara Crooker. Finding new ways to feel tranquil gives us more compassion, contentment, and appreciation for our blessings.

"The Serenity Prayer" encourages us to accept the things we cannot change and to muster the courage to change the things we can. May the selections in *Serenity Prayers* provide the encouragement and inspiration you need to practice the profound thoughts in this deeply moving prayer.

— June Cotner
P.O. Box 2765
Poulsbo, WA 98370
june@junecotner.com
www.junecotner.com

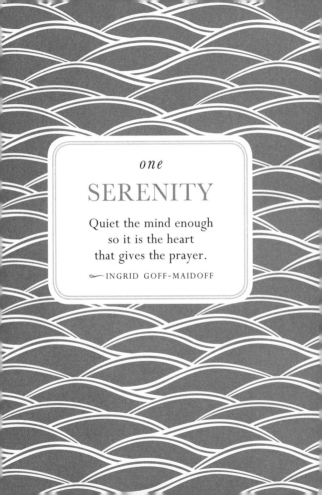

one

SERENITY

Quiet the mind enough
so it is the heart
that gives the prayer.

— INGRID GOFF-MAIDOFF

JOY

You speak to me
in the silence,
Your voice the chinook.
You heal me
in the beauty
of the pine forests.
I am filled
with Your presence
in the gentle fall
of snow on a mountain trail.
Blessed, by the incense of Your flowers.

Joy is mine
to see the eagle in flight
feathers curled upward
catching thermals.
Your beneficence
is everywhere, if only
I have the eyes
to see.

∽ SHIRLEY KOBAR

WELCOMING ANGELS

In the arduous simplicity of this moment
I open my heart, mind, and soul to stillness.
In the deeper quiet
I sense the greater Life that is my life.
I do not live only; I am lived.
I do not breathe only; I am breathed.
I am not only the one I appear to be
but also the One who appears as me.

⟞ RABBI RAMI M. SHAPIRO

A CLEAR MIDNIGHT

This is thy hour O Soul, thy free flight into the
    wordless,
Away from books, away from art, the day erased,
    the lesson done,
Thee fully forth emerging, silent, gazing, pondering
    the themes thou lovest best,
Night, sleep, death and the stars.

— WALT WHITMAN
   (1819–1892)

LET US SPEND ONE DAY
AS DELIBERATELY AS NATURE

Let us spend one day as deliberately as Nature,
and not be thrown off the track by every nutshell
and mosquito's wing that falls on the rails. Let us
rise early and fast, or break fast, gently and without
perturbation; let company come and let company
go, let the bells ring and the children cry—
determined to make a day of it . . . If the engine
whistles, let it whistle till it is hoarse for its pains.
If the bell rings, why should we run? . . . Time is
but the stream I go a-fishing in.

⌒ HENRY DAVID THOREAU
(1817–1862)

AN ORDINARY DAY

It was so simple. So average . . .
how could he find perfection in such an
ordinary day . . . I realized this was the
whole point.

⟋ MITCH ALBOM

I MUST WALK AGAIN THE WOODED PATH

I must walk again the wooded path;
   I must stroll the country lane
Where sunsets fall like summer plums
   and stardust falls like rain.

I must chase again the firefly
   on the honeysuckle vine.
And watch an eagle spread its wings
   above the tallest pine.

I must see once more a hummingbird
   where hollyhocks grow wild.
And run barefoot through Autumn leaves
   like I did as a child.

I must stand atop a mountain
   when the valley's white with snow.
And linger there till purple haze
   spreads twilight far below.

I must do these things lest I forget
   how precious life can be.
I must walk again the wooded path
   of quaint simplicity.

∾ CLAY HARRISON

THE GIFT I GIVE MYSELF

Our voices turn so easily into
too much noise.
The gift I give myself
is a day of silence so that I might
retrieve what has been lost in the clamor—
of cars, the frenzy, the gossip—
what we mistake for connection.

In silence, I watch the leaves,
each crimson and tangerine hue
more brilliant than the next on its slow descent—
as if a message is there for the reading.
In silence, I hear the wind
crackling its own stormy song.
In silence, I notice
a branch bending in the wind,
as if to lean closer, to whisper in my ear
its timeless secrets.

— JANE BUTKIN WAGNER

WHEN I DANCE, I DANCE

When I dance, I dance; when I sleep, I sleep;
yes, and when I walk alone in a beautiful orchard,
if my thoughts have been dwelling elsewhere,
I bring them back to the walk, the orchard, to the
sweetness of this solitude, and to me.

⌒ MONTAIGNE
(1533-1592)

DROP THY STILL DEWS OF QUIETNESS

Drop Thy still dews of quietness,
Till all our strivings cease;
Take from our souls the strain and stress,
And let our ordered lives confess
The beauty of Thy peace.

— JOHN GREENLEAF WHITTIER
(1807–1892)

LISTEN

Listening
to your heart,
finding out who you are,
is not simple.
It takes time for
the chatter to quiet down.
In the silence of "not doing"
we begin to know
what we feel.
If we listen and hear
what is being offered,
then anything in life
can be our guide.
Listen.

⟜ AUTHOR UNKNOWN

BE STILL

In the rush and noise of life, as you have intervals, step within yourself and be still. Wait upon God and feel his good presence; this will carry you through your day's business.

⟋ WILLIAM PENN
(1644–1718)

MINING THE HEART

Let us kneel
before the stream
of our lives

mining for those
golden moments when
we see right through

to the real: kindness,
laughter, innocence,
the light of all things

Then, slowly
release all the rest
allow it to flow

the way life will when
we learn what to hold,
what to let go

⟜ ARLENE GAY LEVINE

SERENITY IS NOT

Serenity is not
A quiet mountain lake,
Nor a nature preserve
With only the birds for company,
Nor release from responsibility:
For the soul determined to fret and worry
Is little swayed by circumstance.
Serenity can be
Found in a blighted inner city
Where every night is shattered by gunfire,
Or in solitary confinement in a dirty cell,
Or amid the onslaught of a dozen demands,
For the soul that rests in God's peace
Is little swayed by circumstance.

— KATHERINE SWARTS

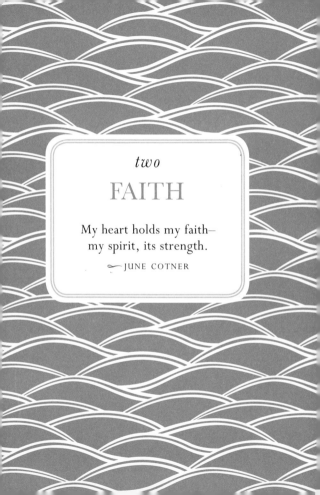

two

FAITH

My heart holds my faith—
my spirit, its strength.

⁓ JUNE COTNER

WHEN I'M WEARY

When I'm weary,
And no longer
Hear Your voice,
I take it up
The mountain
To breathe
Your Blessing
Where pines
Are as tall
As cathedrals,
And silence

Is broken
By footfalls
As I walk
Your aisles
Of well-trodden paths.

⌒ SHIRLEY KOBAR

ANGEL EMBRACE

There are angels who sit quietly
and whisper when we need comfort.
There are those who breathe life into us
when we are breathless.

There are angels who fill us with gracious support
when our souls become fragile,
and those who kiss us goodnight
for a peaceful slumber.

There are angels that touch us with sacred laughter
when tears become a burden.
There are those who wrap their wings around us
and rock us until the ache in our heart disappears.

There are angels that can send us
flying with wonder
when our hope begins to fade,
and those who devote everything to give us
everlasting peace in heaven.

— LORI EBERHARDY

WIN OR LOSE, I WILL SURVIVE

The best way to find myself is to be lost. It's at those times when I'm vulnerable, weak, and scared that I learn the most. In my quest for answers, my search for the right path, I discover who I really am: a courageous soul, a brave warrior, a fighter. And with the help of family, friends, and faith, I finally conquer and find my way. I emerge stronger and have a deeper sense of what makes me special and unique. I know every obstacle is really an opportunity, and that win or lose, I will survive.

— JOANNE HIRASE-STACEY

YOU MUST BELIEVE

You must believe
even when it feels
like there is nothing to believe in.
You must believe with all your heart,
day in and day out, that there
is an unseen spark
readying to turn into a whole constellation
that will fill every corner of your world
with wishes and light.

⌐ CORRINE DE WINTER

RENEWAL

Imagine not that life is all doing.
Stillness, too, is life;
and in that stillness
the mind cluttered with busyness quiets,
the heart reaching to win rests,
and we hear the whispered truths of God.

∽ RABBI RAMI M. SHAPIRO

CONSOLATION

Out of the virgin quiet
God often speaks to me,
Saying I'm ever present,
Consoling me tenderly.

The leaf, the tree, the flower,
The birds that sing in prayer,
Love from friends and family
Tell me God is always there.

— MARION SCHOEBERLEIN

THE KALEIDOSCOPE OF LIFE

Faith is the power
to stand against all odds,
showing conviction in your beliefs.
It is never taking no for an answer.
It is believing without seeing.
Faith is hoping for impossibilities
when your own strength
has been worn down and depleted.
It is never giving up.
It is never giving in.
It is moving on
the kaleidoscope of life
when you don't feel like dancing.
It is winning—
before the race has even begun.

⌒ LESLIE A. NEILSON

LET NOTHING DISTURB YOU

Let nothing disturb you;
Let nothing dismay you.
All things pass;
God never changes.
Patience attains
All it strives for.
The one who has God
Finds that nothing is lacking.
God alone suffices.

∽ SAINT TERESA OF ÁVILA
   (1515–1582)

PRAYER FOR PROTECTION

The light of God surrounds us;
The love of God enfolds us;
The power of God protects us;
The presence of God watches over us;
Wherever we are, God is!

～ JAMES DILLET FREEMAN
   (1912–2003)

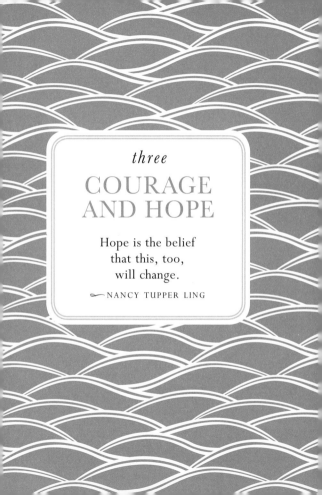

three

COURAGE
AND HOPE

Hope is the belief
that this, too,
will change.

—NANCY TUPPER LING

LIVING IN HOPE

When I feel most alone,
Hope holds my hand.
When sadness buckles me,
Hope helps me stand.
When circumstances overwhelm me,
Hope restores my energy.
When chores numb and bore me,
Hope glorifies them.
When I fear self-revelation,
Hope gives me courage to be myself.

To live in hope is to believe
in light when it is dark,
in beauty when ugliness abounds,
in peace when conflict reigns,
in love when hatred marches.

May I never stop hoping.

〜 SUZANNE C. COLE

HOPE

The faintest of whispers: the softest of sighs,
a "did I see something" obliquely pass by?

a movement that speaks; a presence that loves,
a rustle of gossamer; myriad doves.

not much is required; so little we need,
the smallest of dreams, a mere mustard seed.

a glimpse, or a glimmer, a flicker of light,
a promise of day against vapid night.

hope.

⌒ SUZANNE GROSSER

CONTENTMENT'S RECIPE

To know what really matters,
To have the heart to care,
To find the will to struggle
When burdens we must bear,
To act when it is time to act,
To speak up when we should,
To keep our silence when we feel
That words will do no good,
To take the time to contemplate
Upon Life's sweeter things,
Will mark us with contentment
That love and wisdom brings.

⟋ HILDA LACHNEY SANDERSON

CLIMBING THE JADE MOUNTAIN

(filling out my son's SSI forms)

The Chinese poets tell us
that to start an impossible journey,
you must begin with small steps,
one foot in front of the other
on the rock-hard road. There are
no maps. The mountain gleams
in the afternoon sun. The load grows
increasingly heavy. We
are tired, we are thirsty,
and we want to know
how many dusty miles remain?
The mountain is silent.

All the guidebooks are written
in an ancient language
we don't understand.
When night overtakes us,
we lie down in a dry
river bed, with a stone
for a pillow. Morning
draws her curtains.
We begin again.

⌒ BARBARA CROOKER

BUILDING BRAVERY

Courage is not recklessness,
Nor the ability to laugh at danger
When out of its reach,
For there can be no courage without fear.
Nor is courage something that comes from
    nowhere
Or lives naturally in a few hearts;
It is built over a lifetime
With blocks of love and faithfulness,
Mortared with wisdom
And a willingness to count cost.

∾ KATHERINE SWARTS

YES

So I said yes to everything, yes to the green hills
rolling out ahead, yes to the hayfield tied up in rolls,
yes to the clouds blooming like peonies in the sky's
blue meadow, the long tongue of the road lolling
out before me, yes to the life of travel, yes to the other
life at home, yes to the daisies freckling the ditch,
to the sun pouring down on everything
like Vermeer's milkmaid and her endless
jug of milk, yes to the winds that pulled the clouds
apart like taffy, then turned them into a classroom
of waving hands punched into fists: yes yes yes.

⌒ BARBARA CROOKER

SEEDS

To trust in what I do not understand—
the way flowers follow

with imperceptible grace
the sequence of the day,

to bend at nightfall
like wheat in the wind

or to let go,
like seeds anticipating Spring—

to be still with the stillness
of my body breathing

is to be, perhaps,
like prayer

alive
and vital in the air.

∽ MICHAEL S. GLASER

four

RELAXATION

When the mind becomes quiet,
you feel nourished.

— SWAMI CHIDVILASANANDA

SOMETIMES, IN A
SUMMER MORNING

Sometimes, in a summer morning, having taken my accustomed bath, I sat in my sunny doorway from sunrise till noon, rapt in a revery, amidst the pines and hickories and sumachs, in undisturbed solitude and stillness, while the birds sang around or flitted noiseless through the house, until by the sun falling in at my west window, or the noise of some traveller's wagon on the distant highway, I was reminded of the lapse of time. I grew in those seasons like corn in the night, and they were far better than any work of the hands would have been.

━ HENRY DAVID THOREAU
(1817–1862)

LET YOUR SOUL CREATE A
SANCTUARY

Let your soul create
a sanctuary where
all dreams are possible
and life is grand as God's glory.
The beach stretches
before you.
You are strong as the sea's song.
Whitecaps travel and return.
May you never
feel alone or
lose sight of the
sacred seasons of your soul.

∽ PAULA TIMPSON

WINDCHIMES

I sit and watch the windchimes sing.
Four polished voices of silver.
Each in perfect harmony with the others,
yet content to sing alone.
Nestled within hangs their raison d'être.
A gentle wooden sphere,
smoothed to make friends with the wind.
Yet every strong breeze it cannot resist,
and the chimes sing.

My heart is a windchime . . .
my life is a gentle breeze . . .
and at the center, my soul.
And every day I listen
to see if I am at peace with the wind.

⟜ JOHN S. FANUKO

NO HURRY

My son and I sit
upon the porch swing rocking
in a hushed, gentle breeze
on a warm summer evening.
We watch clouds roll past
the moon and fireflies dance.
We breathe in the moment
with soft, summer sighs.
We rock and we rock.
No words between us.
We are in no hurry
to go in to sleep.
We are dreaming
outdoors tonight.

⌒ SHERRI WAAS SHUNFENTHAL

SANCTUARY

Grab hold of your imagination,
tug on it till it cooperates, and
with its help, create a haven,
your own private sanctuary,
sprinkled in pixie dust, watered
with daydreams. Perhaps,

it is a sheltered garden,
a wooded glen or pebbled beach,
whatever scene nourishes you,
whatever sights and sounds calm
you, whatever regenerates you.

Know that in the blink of an eye,
the tick of a heart's clock,
you can travel there.

Airline tickets aren't necessary.
Road maps can be stored away.
Advanced booking is not required.
The only reservation you need
make is one with yourself.

— SUSAN ROGERS NORTON

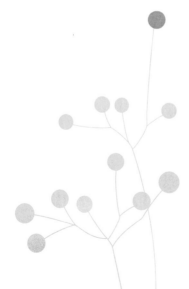

HOW THE ROSE WORKS

I get up—second night of sleeping soundly,
with only one brief awakening—past dawn.
The rose bush, already in the summer sun,
just glows. Some blossoms drying brown
on top, others down below, pinkly hot.
Birds flutter, twit, and sit. But I pay no mind.
My eyes watch the roses as I sip my tea and
feel fine. The rose does her work in silence,
like a writer or a yogi, focused and aware,
moves so slowly you can't see it unless patient
enough to sit for hours with a calm mind,

and simply stare. This is how I want to live
my life, still and balanced, yet always growing,
open to the cycles of bud and blooming,
full of beauty, roots deep, thorns for protection,
stalks strong with liquid flowing up to feed
the bees, emitting sweet perfume into the air.

⌒ CASSIE PREMO STEELE

HAMMOCK

I want to let go
relax into the hammock of myself
let drumbeat of blood

surges of muscle and nerve
and music of breath all rock me
I want to allow

sunlight to spill off my face
and when ponderous clouds
move in dark

and deep as the center of black-
eyed Susans, I want to be present
to the drumming rain

— LINDA GOODMAN ROBINER

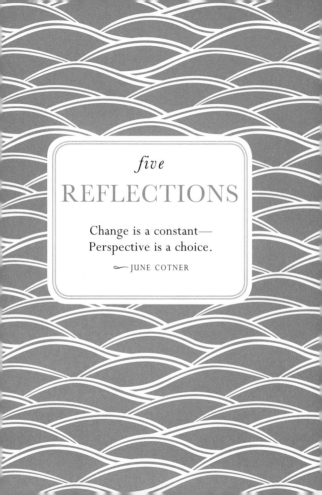

five

REFLECTIONS

Change is a constant—
Perspective is a choice.

— JUNE COTNER

CHASSEURCISTIC

*(Chasseurcistic: of or pertaining to one of a body
of light cavalry or infantry trained for rapid maneuvering.)*

Sometimes we must be reminded to leave translation
    loose, not bind it too literally.
Otherwise, we miss the little miracles, the tiny rushes
that come from walking in a blush-sky sunset,
or drinking in an ocean full of diamonds and green
    glass,
or sleeping in the essence of a lover's post-coital sigh.
Our ears are trained daily to hear marketing tips,
societal status, individual worth; yet, we must not
    forget
to listen, too, to the laughter of tree tops dancing
    with the wind
to the music of sun-bath and moon-wash.

Our eyes are accustomed to four-lane traffic,
with instinct sharpened for advantage, the sliver of
    opportunity;
but, we must remember to soothe away redness
with healing drops of Earth in spring renewal,
with ointment of colors in all their natural splendor,
and the cooling lotion of ocean waves
writing their eternal promise against the caramel
    sands.
The challenge is to take life as it really is.

↜ MARIAN LOVENE GRIFFEY

THE WORLD WE MAKE

We make the world in which we live
By what we gather and what we give,
By our daily deeds and the things we say,
By what we keep or we cast away.

We make our world by the beauty we see
In a skylark's song or a lilac tree,
In a butterfly's wing, in the pale moon's rise,
And the wonder that lingers in midnight skies.

We make our world by the life we lead,
By the friends we have, by the books we read,
By the pity we show in the hour of care,
By the loads we lift and the love we share.

We make our world by the goals we pursue,
By the heights we seek and the higher view,
By hopes and dreams that reach the sun
And a will to fight till the heights are won.

What is the place in which we dwell,
A hut or a palace, a heaven or hell,
We gather and scatter, we take and we give,
We make our world—and there we live.

— ALFRED GRANT WALTON
(1887–1970)

SUCCESS

Success
has less to do
   with the accumulation
     of things,

And more to do
   with the stringing together
     of significant moments,

Important times spent
   with those we love,
Memories cherished
    by those who love us.

— SUSAN ROGERS NORTON

FORGIVENESS

Take me back
to the beginning.
Wrap a peace which falls
like sheer rain
between the folds of petals,
under blades of grass,
between unanswered questions,
underneath the doubt,
the pain, ripe and raw,
pungent as memory,
sweet as forgiveness.

⌒ LALITA NORONHA

IS IT SO SMALL A THING

From the *Hymn of Empedocles*

Is it so small a thing
To have enjoy'd the sun,
To have lived light in the spring,
To have loved, to have thought, to have done;
To have advanced true friends, and beat down
   baffling foes . . .

∿ MATTHEW ARNOLD
   (1822–1888)

PASSION

I think people don't place a high enough value on how much they are nurtured by doing whatever it is that totally absorbs them. Whenever people are totally caught up in what they are doing—their passion—a timeless quality exists in which they are expressing the real essence of their authentic self. And this genuine essence, this authentic self, thereby helps their inner love grow.

⤙ JEAN SHINODA BOLEN

REQUIEM FOR MY SISTER

When the end
comes,
in its dark
and mysterious
colors,
we stand tall
as we can,
and the sun
slips out
from behind
the cloud
and sheds
its long light
back over our time,
and we marvel
at where we've been,

the sum
of our days,
who we became,
the gifts
that were given,
and quietly
we return
to the sea,
from which
all things come,
rejoicing
in the night,
twinkling
like a star.

⌒ GARY HANNA

THE LAME GOAT

You've seen a herd of goats
going down to the water.

The lame and dreamy goat
brings up the rear.

There are worried faces about that one,
but now they're laughing,

because look, as they return,
that goat is leading!

There are many different kinds of knowing.
The lame goat's kind is a branch
that traces back to the roots of presence.

Learn from the lame goat,
and lead the herd home.

⟋ RUMI
(1207–1273)
TRANSLATED BY COLEMAN BARKS

OF CONSEQUENCE

It is not what we know
that really matters,
but what we do
with what we know.

It is not how strong we are
that means anything,
but how much willpower we have
to use that strength wisely
when it is needed.

And it is not how kind
or faithful and prayerful we are
in our thoughts and intentions
that makes any real difference,
but how we let that inner goodness
reach out and touch others.

Wisdom, strength, and goodness
are only meaningful
when well-used,
and that is the essence of
what really is
of any consequence.

⌒ HILDA LACHNEY SANDERSON

IT WILL PASS

"It will pass,"
my grandfather said to me on his dying bed.
He meant the moment.
He meant my concerns.
He meant his life.
And in that glimmering instant
of Truth
I felt the universe sigh—
And ready again,
to take another breath.

～ AIMÉE CARTIER

UNCONDITIONAL DIVIDENDS

I remember
to embrace
love
in all its forms,
especially
when
I forget love
always
flows back to me
after the giving time
falls away.

∾ JOAN NOËLDECHEN

I SAW THAT IT WAS GOOD

Walking through the breezeway into the parking lot at my church the other day brought me face to beak with a beautiful red male cardinal. He startled me as he darted from a small tree to the ground for a few seconds and back to the tree. Parked to my immediate right was a small, attractive, bright red sports car . . . a convertible, yet! It was a beautiful tribute to modern engineering and creative ability, but it couldn't compare with the Creator's creature. The cardinal was vibrant, alive; in freedom he was able to fly, to investigate, to care for his young family, to live the life lovingly given him. His bright red color was even a distraction for the female's protection. The convertible "red bird" looked like fun, but was no match for the beautiful bird.

Perhaps in those few seconds of comparison, I was being reminded that too often I take God's creation and love for granted. Sometimes the shiny, enticing "things" of this world draw us in and we miss the real beauty all around us.

Maybe I should take up bird-watching!

⌁ BETTY ANN LEAVITT

REALIZATIONS

Sometimes life is hard.
Possibilities are impossible.
Understanding is misunderstood.
Hope is hopeless.

But every belief I have and
Everything I've learned in life
Leads to this:

There are others in the world
With bigger mountains to climb
With bigger oceans to swim
With bigger divides to cross.

My mountains are speed bumps in the road
My oceans are narrow streams
My divides are cracks in the sidewalk.

I am blessed beyond measure
I am abounding in love
I am lucky to be me.

⌒ JOANNE HIRASE-STACEY

ENIGMA

Maybe the reason we can't capture joy
is that it comes in pieces
>   a forgiveness granted
>   an accident avoided
>   a friendship deepened
>   a gratitude spoken
>   a talent discovered
>   a natural wonder witnessed
>   a difficult concept mastered
>   a goal attained
>   a love recovered

that must be put together like a puzzle
and appreciated like a beautiful picture,
unfolding.

— JANICE M. JONES

CLOUDS THAT PASS

It is not the last word,
nor the accumulation of material things,
nor the deadline we could not meet
that matter.
These are earthly things,
transient, temporary.
When we dwell on these
it is to no purpose.
They are like clouds that pass in a blue sky,
changing but always present,
For a short time
Blocking the light and the knowledge
That we are part of the divine.

⌒ CORRINE DE WINTER

THE SONGS ALONG THE WAY

Some people chase forever
The gold at rainbow's end.
Some never hear a bird sing
Nor the laughter of a friend.
Some search for fields of velvet;
Not watching where they pass.
Some never see a sunrise
Nor the daisies in the grass.
They're always looking elsewhere
For some better day
When it's always right beside them
In the songs along the way.

— JOAN STEPHEN

six

JOY AND
GRATITUDE

Let gratitude
   in the evening
      bring you joy
         in the morning.

⟶ JUNE COTNER

THE CUP OF LIFE

Take this cup,
I've filled it up,
with love and joy and laughter.
Now it's empty,
Fill it up.
Repeat,
Forever after.
First, so full
I'm giving
All my love and joy in living.
Then near empty,
Tired of living,
And I'm the
One who needs the giving.

This cup, this cup,
this cup of life,
It's always overflowing;
We give and get
And get and give,
Life's balance
Keeps on going.
Take this cup,
I've filled it up,
With love and joy and laughter.
Now it's empty,
Fill it up.
Repeat,
Forever, after.

— LAURA BYRNES

LISTEN,

I want to tell you something. This morning
is bright after all the steady rain, and every iris,
peony, rose, opens its mouth, rejoicing.
I want to say, wake up, open your eyes,
there's a snow-covered road ahead, a field
of blankness, a sheet of paper, an empty screen.
Even the smallest insects are singing, vibrating
their entire bodies, tiny violins of longing
and desire. We were made for song.

I can't tell you what prayer is, but I can take
the breath of the meadow into my mouth,
and I can release it for the leaves' green need.
I want to tell you your life is a blue coal, a slice
of orange in the mouth, cut hay in your nostrils.
The cardinals' red song dances in your blood.
Look, every month the moon blossoms
into a peony, then shrinks to a sliver of garlic.
And then it blooms again.

⌒ BARBARA CROOKER

NEVERTHELESS;

And in spite of, everything,
we are. Here.

Once. Our time
is short, the flare

of a candle,
the pulse

of a heart. Swirl
the wine

in your glass.
Put on

a necklace
of sky. Invite

the neighbors. Dance.

∽ BARBARA CROOKER

HUMILITY

The kitchen floor needs sweeping
where the dust devils swirl
by the door where the cats tuck and curl.
It never lets up, dishes in the sink,
stacked up like the steady stream of days.
And every Tuesday, without fail,
you haul the garbage to the curb.

You do this work not because it keeps you
from doing something greater,
like reading a book, taking pleasure
in simply holding the words and turning
each page, or staring out the window
at gathering grey river clouds, seeing
for the first time at the edge of town,
fields of tender wheat.

It's the daily humbling that's required.
A clipping of wings to ground
you to what's needed.
And if for a moment you pause,
soft hands glistening in rainbows
of soap suds, a pile of swept wood
shavings and crumbs at your feet,
think of yourself as lucky,
anticipate the approach of rain
against the panes of glass,
listen as the cats do
with a twitch of an ear
and count, one by one,
these blessings of home.

⌒ STEPHEN J. LYONS

GRAVY

Every day on this earth
is gravy. Gravy

ladled over every last
thing. Lay it on thick. Lick

the plate when you're through
eating. Don't leave

anything leftover. Tomorrow
will always be there

tomorrow. Only today is better
than today. Savor

the smells—the kitchen
before and after.

Chew slow. Taste
every last bite.

∽ PETER MARKUS

PRECIOUS MOMENTS

Rainbows and roses after the rain,
The splendor of twilight embracing the plain . . .
Strolls by the seaside beneath a full moon,
A butterfly's flight from an empty cocoon.
A carpet of leaves of pure autumn gold,
Reflections of love in the young and the old . . .
Blossoms of apple and cherry and plum,
The joy of a child when Christmas has come.
The beauty of sunset setting the hillside aglow,
The wonder and peace of new fallen snow . . .
Bees making honey, the glory of spring,
A mockingbird learning a new song to sing.
The stillness of dawn's pale lavender skies,
The leaping of hearts when a baby first cries . . .
The splendor and grace of an eagle in flight,
The silence of stars guarding the night.

A baby's first step, a daughter's first prayer,
Our flag proudly waving in cool mountain air . . .
A lover's first kiss, a hug from a friend,
It's these precious moments we pray never end.

∾ CLAY HARRISON

TAKE NOTHING FOR GRANTED

Take nothing for granted: the sheer act
of waking each day; fresh air upon your cheek;
each effort expended on self or another—
walking the dog, shopping for food, toiling
at home   in an office   or on the road.
Every moment is rare, short, and full of glory.
Every word is magic, a story achieved through will.
Marvel at nature's moods as mirror of your own.
Recall a sunrise or sunset, a flock of geese in the sky.
Care about parents or children as fragile gifts
like petal on a rose, like song from one bird.

Praise the simple or complex—the invention of flight
above clouds; the wheel; the bathtub; a rocking-chair.
We rise and fall in the moon or a wave,
in a smile or many tears. And being brave
is to be alive as we give and share love
always, only and ever to survive.

⤙ ROCHELLE LYNN HOLT

DAWN'S GRACE

Every morning is a prayer
as the world unfolds to reveal
the ordinary as miracle.

I pray to be a witness to wonder.
To notice that the simplest things
are blessings bestowed.

Right this moment,
I am alive with the gratitude
awareness has granted.

∽ JEAN NICOLE BASS

MY BEAUTIFUL DAY

I borrowed a poem from the sky,
And music from a bird,
I stole a chime out of the wind,
And from the rose a word.
I borrowed a song from the hills,
A psalm from the silver rain,
I took the footsteps of angels
Out of a cobbled lane,
From each little thing I fashioned
Something in my own way.
With God's help I put in my heart
A beautiful, wonderful day!

⟶ MARION SCHOEBERLEIN

GOING THROUGH THE MOTIONS

Going through the motions
I went looking for
the beauty of the moment

as I toiled in the garden
rummaged through the trash
watched suds slip circular
down the drain

the sun descended
as I sat holding my breath,
waiting to turn on any lights,
the evening's glow
resting on my walls

I searched and searched
and ended up finding it
everywhere I looked.

∽ NANCY M. WHITLOCK

GRATITUDE

A morning without work is a morning to breathe,
to watch the rain clear and walk inside the passing
voices of strangers, a dog's barking, students with
their bouncing knapsacks of books, baseball hats
worn backwards, as I walk headed toward nowhere
important, which is, of course, the most important
place of all—the trees dazzling with light, the dog
laps a puddle reflecting the sky, drinking the shimmer,
his belly a puddle of sky, and my feet beginning to
glide down the block, children skipping rope on the
sidewalk, hip hopping to hopscotch calls and double
dutch dance steps, scrawling their names in wet chalk
running colors like a clown's extravagant tears—the
minor miracle of my job, this gathering and giving
of details: a woman's perfume: lilacs and lemons, the
breath of a baby's hair.

⌒ SEAN THOMAS DOUGHERTY

NO LONGER FORWARD NOR BEHIND

No longer forward nor behind
I look in hope or fear;
But, grateful, take the good I find,
the best of now and here.

⁓ JOHN GREENLEAF WHITTIER
(1807–1892)

INVOCATION

Walk out, in an October morning,
the lawn laced with frost and dew,
the sky already burning blue.
Walk into a meadow ringing
with the song of small insects:
"no regrets, no regrets."
Stopper this day with a cork,
pour the sun in a bottle.
Dry goldenrod, thistle, yarrow,
preserve fruit in glass jars,
place them on cellar shelves.

Stop still in your tracks,
watch the sky turn black,
the moon float up like a lucky coin
tossed by the dark trees.
Dance by yourself in the moonlight
spilling like flute music over the lawn.
What more could you possibly ask?

— BARBARA CROOKER

EVERYDAY BLESSINGS

As the years pass, I am coming more and more
to understand that it is the common, everyday
blessings of our common everyday lives for which
we should be particularly grateful. They are the
things that fill our lives with comfort and our hearts
with gladness—just the pure air to breathe and the
strength to breathe it; just warmth and shelter and
home folks; just plain food that gives us strength;
the bright sunshine on a cold day; and a cool
breeze when the day is warm.

⌒ LAURA INGALLS WILDER
(1867–1957)

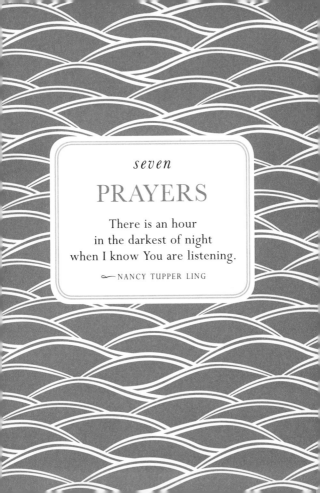

seven

PRAYERS

There is an hour
in the darkest of night
when I know You are listening.

— NANCY TUPPER LING

PSALM FOR THE MEANING OF LIFE

Let me find grace in the real world,
   release in the world of my imagination,
   and joy in both.
Help me to notice the lessons in Your world—
   the turtle to remind me to slow down;
   the peach and the lilac to remind me
      of what in life is sweet;
   the charred piece of driftwood to remind me
      that I, too, have been through the fire;
   the tall yarrow alongside the road
      bending in the wind to remind me
      that I may be bent, but not broken;
   the newborn child to remind me
      that wonder and trust are the hope
      of the future.
Let me have a hope that bears out.

— PHYLLIS K. COLLIER
   (1939–2010)

LIVE QUIETLY

God help us to live quietly
   Amidst the clamor,
      To find that slower pace
          that gentler place
     Where our hearts can listen,
        Where we can listen to
      Our hearts.
        Amen.

— JIM CROEGAERT

POET'S COMPLINE

O Light and Love beyond the darkness,
    carry my words to a peaceful pause,
    my eyes to a rest-filled close.

Breathe open my ear at day
    and bid me rise, a child again,
    to skip barefooted and sure,
    springing with my kite
    in joyful leaps.

Deafen me to all who shout
    there is no Wind.

⟿ DIANNE M. DEL GIORNO

HINDU PRAYER

Grant me, O Master, by thy grace
To follow all the good and pure;
To be content with simple things;
To speak no ill of others;
To have a mind at peace;
Set free from care, and led astray from thee,
Neither by happiness nor woe;
To consider my fellows not as means but ends,
To serve them stalwartly in thought, word and deed;
Never to utter a word of hatred or of shame;
To cast away all selfishness and pride.

Set thou my feet upon this path,
And keep me steadfast in it:
Thus only shall I please thee, serve thee right.

— GOSWAMI TULSIDAS
(1532–1623)

A PRAYER OF THANKSGIVING

We have so much to be thankful for when we
remember our reasons for gratitude—the blessings
we may take for granted, the blessings we would miss
bitterly if they vanished.

So we thank the Creator for:
partners who love, protect, and empower us,
friends who share our lives in tragedy and triumph,
children who model bliss, living in the present,
    and the joy of creation,
people who smile at us for no apparent reason,
those who do their jobs every day so that our lives
    can be easier and more comfortable,

those who practice consideration and politeness,
all the experiences and lessons which help us grow,
   even the painful ones,
the many gifts of nature—cedars and cedar
   waxwings, rain and rainbows, spiders and
   spider lilies,
technology—potable water, air-conditioning,
   central heat, telephones, and computers,
health and the medicines which help us maintain it,
living in the twenty-first century.

We ask Your help in remembering to practice
an attitude of gratitude today and every day.

⌐ SUZANNE C. COLE

PRAYER FOR PERSPECTIVE

Help us to do our best—to strive
for justice and fairness even when
it seems the world around us is mired
in ancient antagonisms. Lend us the wisdom
to cherish each bridge we're able to build
even when it's neither as grand
nor as wide as the span of our dreams
and grant us the grace to trust the future
to forgive us for the things we could not change
as it crosses the rivers we thought impassable.

∼ PEG DUTHIE

ON THIS DAY

God, on this day
I welcome you into my heart.
I ask you for the patience
and wisdom,
for the light and understanding
to help others, to help myself,
to allow me the strength
to make my life worthy and meaningful
as you have intended it to be.

∽ CORRINE DE WINTER

I PRAY TODAY

I pray today for
Those who are homeless to find shelter.
Those who are depressed to discover joy.
Those who are addicted to find release.
Those who are lonely to find a friend.
Those who are confused or lost to find a path.
Those who are heartbroken
to know that it will pass.
Those who are sick to find healing.
Those who live in darkness to be covered in light.
Those who are dying
to know that they have lived.
I pray today for peace where there is unrest,
for love to prevail over all.

⟳ CORRINE DE WINTER

eight

INSPIRATION

Be like the hummingbird:
Gather sweetness in all you do.

— JUNE COTNER

MY SYMPHONY

To live content with small means; to seek elegance rather than luxury, and refinement rather than fashion; to be worthy, not respectable, and wealthy, not rich; to study hard, think quietly, talk gently, act frankly; to listen to stars and birds, to babes and sages, with open heart; to bear all cheerfully, do all bravely, await occasions, hurry never. In a word, to let the spiritual, unbidden and unconscious, grow up through the common. This is to be my symphony.

— WILLIAM HENRY CHANNING
(1810–1884)

EPIPHANY

It was Einstein who said
either nothing is a miracle,
or everything is—
a jagged mountain range,
lilacs in bloom,
a peacock unfurled,
sun on your arm,
the touch of a stranger.

Take your pick: be surprised
by nothing at all,
or by everything that is.

— MARYANNE HANNAN

THE WAY HOME

There is a way home.
It runs through the cornfields beneath the stars,
rises like a river
to wash the apple trees below the barn.
If you are careful you will not disturb the snakes
who curl in the tall weeds
beside the grassy path your feet have known.

Sometimes in the distance
you will see the others,
silhouettes on moonlit hills
carrying hoes over their shoulders,
returning from their fields
even as you go to yours,
sure-footed as a goat
down the stubbled rows toward sleep.

When you climb to the graveyard on the hillside,
stop among the old ones,
take off your clothes,
lie down on the earth
with your head in the shadows
the moon throws between tombstones,
and begin to count the stars
in the Milky Way.

You will run out of numbers.
You will run out of words.
You will forget how to talk to the sky.
You will forget where you have come from,
or where you are going.
You will only know that you are light
among the stars,

and that cornfields spiral out from you
on every side, shining corn
as far as you can see—
even over the edge of the world,
that dark circle you have found
at last.

∽ PENNY HARTER

TOMORROW IS NOT PROMISED

Tomorrow is not promised,
So I will live today
With faith, with joy, in peacefulness,
While death is held at bay.
I will not waste a moment of
Life's offerings and gifts;
These pieces of eternity
I'll use with care and thrift.
And yet I'll not be frugal with
The love that's mine to give.
I'll share with great abandon;
'Tis the only way *to live.*

— SUSANNE WIGGINS BUNCH

THE JOURNEY

A day begins; there are no promises.
Maybe the sun will shine, or not.
No one can be sure who is around that corner
or what news this next call might bring.

Seasons arrive like clockwork but how
they will turn out is a mystery. Still . . .
One day we will slip from our bodies
and slide into the Light; this we know.

Perhaps to rouse from sleep and put aside
the fear that hunts our hearts,
we could live each day
as if the Light was already ours.

Listen: The heart hears a deeper truth
than the head. Even the loneliest
one is never alone on
the winding journey Home.

⌒ ARLENE GAY LEVINE

WRITER'S COLONY, SPRING

Maybe, then, this is heaven, flowering trees
like huge bouquets, even the bushes
festooned with blossoms: lilac,
mock orange, bridal wreath, basket of gold.
Every day, the sun shines, pours in
the studio window, pools on the floor.
Lean on the casement, and a halo settles
around your shoulders. The sky
is an ethereal blue. Here,
all the ticking clocks have wound
down; each day is measured in cups of light.
Appointment books and calendars
have no use, shed like deciduous leaves
in the soft wind. No carping critics
with their detailed whispers of all the ways
you don't measure up. The only sound

is the twitter of birds. And maybe
these birds that fly back and forth
in the hedgerow are really angels,
they open their beaks and whole choruses
tumble out. Can you hear them sing,
"Write it down, write it down?" Head bowed
as any penitent, I confess. I have been
too long away from my desk.
Here, let the song rise in my throat,
come up from underground limestone
caverns, like the small warbling streams
of the Shenandoah, may they run in
rivulets, cascades of melody,
whole laughing brooks of words,
until you cannot tell the singer
from the song.

⌒ BARBARA CROOKER

I CAN BELIEVE IN FAIRIES

I can believe in fairies:
The graceful dragonfly,
The hummingbird in summer,
The breeze that rustles by,
All sing of soft enchantment
That whispers in the air;
Where little things bring beauty
A Fairyland is there.

I can believe in magic:
The rainbow with its arch,
The frost upon my window,
White clouds in breezy March,
All sing of spells and marvels
Surrounding everywhere;
Where hearts can soar in wonder
A magic world is there.

I still believe in angels:
For every loving deed,
Each close escape from danger,
Each meeting of a need,
All sing of heaven's wonders,
Of worship and of prayer;
Where love and hope are dancing
An angel's touch is there.

⟊ KATHERINE SWARTS

AS IF FOREVER . . .

Is not already ours,
we live our little lives
fearful of what was
and what might be
forgetting there is only now
and now is our forever

As if forever . . .
were a place one could
get to by being good
or wishing or holding on
with a tight fist and pouf!
there you are

As if forever . . .
were something other than
the being, the breath, the seeing
what is right in front of you
and knowing this moment
is all we need

— ARLENE GAY LEVINE

I BELIEVE

I believe in miracles and dreams that will come true.
I believe in tender moments and friendship, through
    and through.

I believe in stardust and moonbeams all aglow.
I believe there's magic and more there than we know.

I believe in reaching out and touching from the heart.
I believe that if we touch a gift we can impart.

I believe that if you cry your tears are not in vain.
And when you're sad and lonely, others know your
    pain.

I believe that when we laugh a sparkle starts to shine.
And I just know that spark will spread from more
    hearts than just mine.

I believe that hidden in the quiet of the night,
there's magic moths, and gypsies, a fairy, and a sprite.

I believe that if you dance the dances of your heart,
that greater happiness will find a brand new way to
    start.

I believe the gifts you have are there for you to share.
And when you give them from the heart, the whole
    world knows you care.

I believe that if you give, even just to one,
that gift will grow in magnitude before the day is
    done.

I believe that comfort comes from giving part of me.
And if I share with others, there's more for all to see.

I believe that love is still the greatest gift of all,
and when it's given from the heart then not one of
    us will fall.

~ AUTHOR UNKNOWN

IT'S ALL GOOD

Life lessons can be disguised in many different ways.

Family and friends are valuable gifts.

Each day really does matter.

Letting go is not the same as surrendering.

It makes a difference to believe in a God.

Tolerance is good but acceptance is better.

It's good to have moments when your faith is tested;
it can only get stronger through exercise.

Having people in your life
that love you unconditionally is necessary.

Giving love back is essential.

Generosity is a noble quality
of a compassionate soul.

To be reminded of the things
that really matter is good, and
to put aside the things that don't is priceless.

The human heart
has an unbelievable capacity to love.

In the dark and the silence you are never alone.

It's all good.

⌐ LORI EBERHARDY

THE GIFT

This new day is a gift—
I open my eyes.
It looks beautiful
wrapped with Your Love,
full of possibilities—
and I haven't even
taken off the ribbons.

I'll open it slowly
during the day
sure to find—
people to love,
things to laugh at,
and places where the touch of my hand
can make a difference.

∽ ZORAIDA RIVERA MORALES

PIPPA'S SONG

The year's at the spring
and the day's at the morn;
Morning's at seven;
The hillside's dew-pearled;
The lark's on the wing;
The snail's on the thorn;
God's in his heaven—
All's right with the world.

~ ROBERT BROWNING
    (1812–1889)

AUTHOR INDEX

Albom, Mitch 7

Arnold, Matthew 58

Barks, Coleman 62

Bass, Jean Nicole 90

Bolen, Jean Shinoda 59

Browning, Robert 129

Bunch, Susanne Wiggins 115

Byrnes, Laura 76

Cartier, Aimée 66

Channing, William Henry 110

Cole, SuzAnne C. 32, 104

Collier, Phyllis K. 100

Cotner, June 19, 51, 75, 109

Croegaert, Jim 101

Crooker, Barbara 36, 39, 78, 80, 96, 118

Del Giorno, Dianne M. 102

De Winter, Corrine 25, 73, 107, 108

Dougherty, Sean Thomas 94

Duthie, Peg 106

Eberhardy, Lori 22, 126

Fanuko, John S. 44

Freeman, James Dillet 30

Glaser, Michael S. 40

Goff-Maidoff, Ingrid 1

Griffey, Marian Lovene 52

Grosser, Suzanne 34

Hanna, Gary 60

Hannan, Maryanne 111

Harrison, Clay 8, 86

Harter, Penny 112

Hirase-Stacey, Joanne 24, 70

Holt, Rochelle Lynn 88

Jones, Janice M. 72

Kobar, Shirley 2, 20

Leavitt, Betty Ann 68

Levine, Arlene Gay 16, 116, 122

Ling, Nancy Tupper 31, 99

Lyons, Stephen J. 82

Markus, Peter 84

Montaigne 12

Neilson, Leslie A. 28

Noëldechen, Joan 67

Noronha, Lalita 57

Norton, Susan Rogers 46, 56

Penn, William 15

Rivera Morales, Zoraida 128

Robiner, Linda Goodman 50

Rumi 62

Sanderson, Hilda Lachney
35, 64

Schoeberlein, Marion 27, 91

Shapiro, Rabbi Rami M. 4, 26

Shunfenthal, Sherri Waas 45

Steele, Cassie Premo 48

Stephen, Joan 74

Swami Chidvilasananda 41

Swarts, Katherine 18, 38, 120

Teresa of Ávila, Saint 29

Thoreau, Henry David 6, 42

Timpson, Paula 43

Tulsidas, Goswami 103

Wagner, Jane Butkin 10

Walton, Alfred Grant 54

Whitlock, Nancy M. 92

Whitman, Walt 5

Whittier, John Greenleaf 13,
95

Wilder, Laura Ingalls 98

PERMISSIONS AND ACKNOWLEDGMENTS

Grateful acknowledgment is made to the authors and publishers for the use of the following material. Every effort has been made to contact original sources. If notified, the publisher will be pleased to rectify an omission in future editions.

Bantam Doubleday Dell Publishing Group, Inc. for "The World We Make" by Alfred Grant Walton from *Poems That Touch the Heart*, edited by A. L. Alexander. Copyright © 1941, 1956 by Doubleday, a division of Bantam Doubleday Dell Publishing Group, Inc.

Coleman Barks for "The Lame Goat" from *The Essential Rumi*, translated by Coleman Barks with John Moyne. Copyright © 1995 by Coleman Barks. Published by HarperSanFrancisco. Permission to reprint granted by Coleman Barks. www.ColemanBarks.com

Jean Nicole Bass for "Dawn's Grace."

Jean Shinoda Bolen for "Passion" from *Handbook for the Heart* by Richard Carlson and Benjamin Shield (Little, Brown, © 1996). Reprinted with permission of Jean Shinoda Bolen. www.JeanBolen.com

Susanne Wiggins Bunch for "Tomorrow Is Not Promised."

Laura Byrnes for "The Cup of Life."

Aimée Cartier for "It Will Pass." www.spreadingblessings.com

SuzAnne C. Cole for "Living in Hope" and "A Prayer of Thanksgiving."

Robert E. Collier for "Psalm for the Meaning of Life" by Phyllis K. Collier.

June Cotner for "Be like the hummingbird," "Change is a constant," "Let gratitude in the evening," and "My heart holds my faith." www.JuneCotner.com

Jim Croegaert for "Live Quietly." www.RoughStonesMusic.com

Barbara Crooker for "Climbing the Jade Mountain," "Invocation," "Listen," "Nevertheless;," "Writer's Colony, Spring," and "Yes." www.BarbaraCrooker.com

Corrine De Winter for "Clouds That Pass," "I Pray Today," "On This Day," and "You Must Believe." www.CorrineDeWinter.com

Dianne M. Del Giorno for "Poet's Compline."

Sean Thomas Dougherty for "Gratitude."

Peg Duthie for "Prayer for Perspective." www.nashpanache.com

Lori Eberhardy for "Angel Embrace" and "It's All Good."

John S. Fanuko for "Windchimes."

Michael S. Glaser for "Seeds." www.MichaelSGlaser.com

Ingrid Goff-Maidoff for "Quiet the mind." www.IngridGoffMaidoff.com

Marian Lovene Griffey for "Chasseurcistic."

Suzanne Grosser for "Hope."

Gary Hanna for "Requiem for My Sister."

Maryanne Hannan for "Epiphany." www.MHannan.com

Clay Harrison for "I Must Walk Again the Wooded Path" and "Precious Moments."

Penny Harter for "The Way Home" from *Turtle Blessing* by Penny Harter (La Alameda Press, 1996). Copyright © 1996 by Penny Harter. Reprinted with permission of the author. www.2hweb.net/penhart

Joanne Hirase-Stacey for "Realizations" and "Win or Lose, I Will Survive."

Rochelle Lynn Holt for "Take Nothing for Granted." www.angelfire.com/blues2/rlynnholt

Janice M. Jones for "Enigma."

Shirley Kobar for "Joy" and "When I'm Weary."

Betty Ann Leavitt for "I Saw That It Was Good."

Arlene Gay Levine for "As If Forever . . . ," "The Journey," and

"Mining the Heart." www.ArleneGayLevine.com

Nancy Tupper Ling for "Hope is the belief" and "There is an hour." www.NancyTupperLing.com

Stephen J. Lyons for "Humility."

Peter Markus for "Gravy."

Leslie A. Neilson for "The Kaleidoscope of Life."

Joan Noëldechen for "Unconditional Dividends." www.myspace.com/writingspaces

Lalita Noronha for "Forgiveness." www.LalitaNoronha.com

Susan Rogers Norton for "Sanctuary" and "Success."

Zoraida Rivera Morales for "The Gift."

Linda Goodman Robiner for "Hammock." www.WriterHelper.com

Hilda Lachney Sanderson for "Contentment's Recipe" and "Of Consequence."

Marion Schoeberlein for "Consolation" and "My Beautiful Day."

Seer Green Press for "Everyday Blessings" by Laura Ingalls Wilder, edited by Stephen W. Hines, from *Saving Graces: The Inspirational Writings of Laura Ingalls Wilder.* www.LiteraryProspector.com

Rabbi Rami M. Shapiro for "Renewal" and "Welcoming Angels." www.RabbiRami.com

Sherri Waas Shunfenthal for "No Hurry."

Cassie Premo Steele for "How the Rose Works." www.CassiePremoSteele.com

Joan Stephen for "The Songs Along the Way."

Katherine Swarts for "Building Bravery," "I Can Believe in Fairies," and "Serenity Is Not."

Paula Timpson for "Let Your Soul Create a Sanctuary." www.PaulasPoetryWorld.blogspot.com

Jane Butkin Wagner for "The Gift I Give Myself."

Nancy M. Whitlock for "Going Through the Motions."

ABOUT THE AUTHOR

June Cotner is the author or editor of thirty books, including the best-selling *Graces, Bedside Prayers,* and *Dog Blessings.* Her books altogether have sold more than one million copies. June's latest love and avocation is giving presentations on adopting prisoner-trained shelter dogs. In 2011, she adopted Indy, a chocolate lab/Doberman mix (a LabraDobie!), from the Freedom Tails program at Stafford Creek Corrections Center in Aberdeen, Washington. June works with Indy daily to build on the wonderful obedience skills he mastered in the program. She and Indy have appeared on the television shows *AM Northwest* in Portland, Oregon, and *New Day Northwest* in Seattle.

A graduate of the University of California at Berkeley, June is the mother of two grown children and lives in Poulsbo, Washington, with her husband. Her hobbies include yoga, hiking, and playing with her two grandchildren.

For more information, please visit June's Web site at www.JuneCotner.com.